Finance 'n *Stilettos*

Money Matters
for the Well-Heeled Woman

By Zaneilia Harris, CFP®

First published by Dog Ear Publishing
4011 Vincennes Rd
Indianapolis, IN 46268
www.dogearpublishing.net

ISBN: 978-1-4575-4157-5

This book is printed on acid-free paper.

Printed in the United States of America

Table of Contents

Foreword

*T*his book was written for the divas who know it all and for those of us who wish we did.

It translates financial jargon and makes finance talk more meaningful and easier to understand. It also gives us "permission" to ask questions and confess what we don't understand.

Zaneilia has always been one to share her knowledge, and she does it so beautifully in this book. As an Empowerment Coach, motivational speaker, and author, I am honored to call Zaneilia my friend and supporter, and I am delighted that the information in this book will help others put their finances in order so we can all be comfortable in our stilettos and walk tall with confidence.

Finance 'n Stilettos reminds us to start where we are and move forward with purpose.

Marsha Haygood
StepWise Associates, LLC
Coauthor of "The Little Black Book of Success"

Acknowledgements

I would like to thank my grandmother, Pattie Smith, for her support and encouragement. I love you so much for raising me and providing me with a good foundation built around love and spiritual guidance. My life wouldn't be what it is if it weren't for you being a part of it.

My husband, Stanley "Chris" Harris, Jr., you have always been a great listener when I share my ideas. I appreciate your insight and support. I couldn't have done this without you. Thank you!

For my daughter, Madison Harris, you are such a blessing to me. I dedicate this book to you. You are the reason I continue to push forward. You are my legacy and I want to pass along my knowledge, guidance, and wisdom so you will be the best young lady you can be.

My aunt, Carolyn Plummer, you have been my rock. Whenever I became discouraged, you would pray for me and give me your wisdom for overcoming the challenges I faced.

To my godmother, Juanita Taylor. Thank you. I truly appreciate having you in my life and your being there in times when I couldn't go to anyone else.

Diane Brown, you have become a wonderful friend to me. I truly look at you like a sister. Thanks for listening and providing objective feedback regarding my life and professional decisions. You never judge, you just support.

Love my support system!

INTRODUCTION

Finance 'n Stilettos:
The Best of Both Worlds

A special kind of magic happens when a woman slides her feet into a beautiful pair of high-heel shoes. She stands taller. Her curves are more pronounced. She is instantly more confident—as long as the shoes fit properly and don't make her feet plead for mercy! Those heels, especially stilettos, impact the way women walk, the way we move, the way we carry ourselves. They give us a boost of self-assurance. It's very similar to the empowerment that comes from being an authority over your personal finances.

Many women, successful and educated, put-together and accomplished, understand professional power and influence but may not take full advantage of the power and influence they have over their money. They're juggling so many responsibilities that if something has to fall off their list of priorities, it's going to be that one thing they don't understand, or the thing they don't want to deal with in the first place. I'm guilty of it myself. If it's something I don't enjoy, I'm not enthusiastic about getting it done—so it's pushed to the bottom of my to-do's, in some cases over and over and over again. I have encountered women who've found the one thing they don't enjoy or have time for is money management, specifically investing toward their future, because balancing home and career is their priority. It takes a backseat until a major life transition, such as retirement, divorce, or death of a spouse, forces it to the forefront. Don't procrastinate; outsource the task to a CERTIFIED FINANCIAL PLANNER™ (CFP®) professional who can help you build your financial support structure. Make this a priority because your future depends on it.

Finance touches every aspect of our lives. The financial services industry represents 7.9%, or $1.24 trillion, of the U.S. gross domestic product.[1] That's why there's such an abundance of information about it everywhere. There are books and blogs, websites and webinars, conferences

[1] (Financial Services Industry in the United States, n.d.)

and consultations. It's very important. And we're surrounded by it, sometimes getting what we need, sometimes being overwhelmed by the numbers, but most often feeling a little confused about the best decisions for our families and our futures.

For some people, money isn't all that exciting unless they're spending it or making it. At least talking about it isn't very exciting. Admit it: You tune out after about 30 seconds of listening to some finance expert whose voice very quickly starts to sound like the adults in an old Charlie Brown cartoon. Wah wah wah wah. Pay down debt. Wah wah wah wah. Max out your savings. Wah wah wah wah. Live beneath your means. Wah wah wah wah.

Believe me, I completely understand. But dry or not, discussing money is important. Here's an example of why: My first job out of college was as an auditor with the federal government. I was making $25,000 a year—a higher salary than some people in my family had ever seen—so naturally my relatives came to me to borrow money. I was single, I didn't have any kids, and as far as they were concerned, my income didn't have responsibilities like theirs did. Others had helped me out along the way, so I felt obligated to return the favor. When my cousin asked me to cosign a car loan, against my better judgment, I agreed. That was a mistake. A big one.

A valuable lesson

You probably can guess what happened. Yes, he defaulted on the loan. Yes, I was stuck with the payments *and* the car. Yes, I felt hurt, frustrated, and betrayed. I had two options: Take over the $5,000 bank note or blemish my credit report, and I didn't want to do either. Fresh out of college on an entry-level salary, I had to cough up an extra $200 a month, which, to someone who has just graduated and is establishing herself in the real world, is a lot of money. (It's a lot of money to some people who are already established, too.)

That experience taught me how to say no to lending money, even to the people I care about and love. It freed me up from feeling like I owed something to everybody. It also allowed me to focus on the importance of financial management, for myself, and now, for my clients. I've learned other valuable lessons in finance, some in the classroom, most through the education of life, but that was one of the greatest.

The first step to becoming financially empowered is asking yourself the hard questions: What do you want your finances to do for you now? In five years? In 15 years? In 30 years? What are you willing to do in order for those things to come to fruition? Really take time to think about it. Don't base your answers on what you feel like you're *supposed to* say. Be real with yourself, the self you are now and the one you aspire to be in the future. Armed with this information, start finding the answers.

Why I wrote this book

I wrote this book for women of all financial statuses, from the ones who've achieved professional success to those who are just starting out in their careers. I am looking to empower women and let them know there is truly a difference between having money in the bank and building wealth. My intention is to make all the moving parts of finance easier to understand, translate industry jargon into plain language, and relate the un-sexiness of money management to the stylishness of something we all love: shoes. You're embarking on a financial renaissance. I want to empower you to leverage all of the opportunities that informed investing can create for you, such as portfolio growth, hedging strategies, legacy protection, and impact and angel investing.

You've already been able to pay your monthly bills, set money aside for your future, and enjoy personal luxuries like spa trips, fine art, and relaxing vacations. You're not starting from ground zero; in most circles you have achieved the ultimate in professional and personal success. You need guidance to pull all the pieces together so you can ensure your future is secure. This book is for you.

Are you one of those women who won't discuss your finances because you don't want anyone to know that you need guidance to better position yourself for the future? This book is for you.

Are you one of those women who have a powerful title and a string of degrees but feel that when you've sought help in the past you were talked down to or belittled just because you were a woman? This book is for you.

Are you one of those women who feel that your current retirement savings aren't enough to support the lifestyle you've worked so hard to achieve? This book is for you.

Do you look the part, dress to kill, and drive a car that screams success but, when you pull back all the layers of your façade, you're unsure how to handle the many aspects of your finances alone? This book is for you.

Have you done all the right things toward maximizing the amount you set aside for your saving and investing, and now you want to ensure you are making all the right choices to increase your portfolio's growth potential? This book is for you.

Are you a recent graduate, new to the workforce with no idea where to begin and feel faint at the idea of starting? Guess what? This book is for you, too.

Finance can be fun. This is not a typo. Finance can seriously be fun. You can even reward yourself when you achieve your goals. Sometimes reaching the goal itself is reward enough because it makes the sacrifice worthwhile. Sometimes you need a little something extra to smile at when you've done a good job being financially responsible. Now, I didn't say you should go out and do something crazy. Be sensible. (Hint: Adding a shoe investment to your wardrobe can be a professional asset *and* make you feel good at the same time!) Do what works to stay encouraged and motivated as you move toward your best financial life. And, of course, keep reading.

I want to answer the questions you have about where you are right now in your finances and where you ultimately would like to be. I want you to be equipped and prepared to meet with financial planners and other professionals in the business of managing money so you can speak with authority and ask knowledgeable questions. I want you to learn and apply that information to your finances and share it with the people you love—especially other women—to help spread the empowerment. I want you to tailor what you learn specifically to yourself and your needs and where you are trying to go. Most of all, I want you to financially free yourself.

The road to wealth

There's a difference between having money in the bank and building wealth. What I want to do here is affirm what you already know and support you in learning more. The conversation about finance, especially when it's directed to or about women, is typically polluted with negativity. It's "You're doing this wrong" or "These are the mistakes you're making." In your relationship with your money, just as in any other relationship, you don't want to be bombarded with the bad stuff. It doesn't encourage us to do anything new—in fact, it can make us feel hopeless and tempt us to shut down. In my practice, it's been more beneficial to move forward toward goals than backtrack to revisit mistakes. The stability of financial security is a great motivator.

We can trace where our beliefs, ideas, and fears about money come from. They're adopted and absorbed from our experiences and become tied to our core values and what's important to us. My professional philosophy about finance is based on empowerment, but I'll share my personal stories about where my money habits come from and what they taught me (like the hard-learned cosigning lesson). In some cases, I needed to get to a healthier place about money and how I viewed it. We all have something to learn. This is a no-judgment zone.

Countless Americans compromise their financial future because of money mistakes they could have strategically avoided. I've done it. You've done it. The good news? It can be undone and stay that way. You can improve your financial behaviors and habits and master strategies that will optimize your investments. We have six chapters to discuss how to do it, and every now and then I'll throw in a little visual stimulation in the form of some very sleek and fantastic shoes. For me, and hopefully for you, that's the best of both worlds.

CHAPTER 1

Strutting in Sandals:
Walk Your Financial Journey

I began wearing heels as a teenager. At that time stilettos weren't the trend, but 3-inch heels were. I loved my heels; they made me feel put together and confident. It was the beginning of my love affair with stylish shoes. It foreshadowed who I was becoming, a young lady with dreams and very few doubts. I could conquer the world. I knew that the foundation of achieving my dreams was learning how to be a good steward of my finances. Thus began my personal financial journey.

I started learning about money when I was a child, but not in the same way most kids do. My grandmother raised me by herself in Kenbridge, Virginia, a small tobacco-growing farming town that has a total of *three* (count 'em: one, two, three) stoplights. You're doing good for yourself there if you're taking care of the bills every month and maybe buying a house. I don't know if Grandma thought about anything beyond that. To her, the money you saved ultimately went to paying the bills. Building savings wasn't much of an option, much less a priority. Most of the people in Kenbridge thought that way. Their joy didn't come from material things, so financially, they were just getting by. I don't come from a family of extreme spenders or savers. I come from a family that tried to pay their bills on time and meet their financial obligations every month the best way they could.

When I was eight years old, my grandmother asked me if I thought she should take my father to court for child support. I don't know why she was having such an adult conversation with me at my age, but I remember telling her no. If he wasn't going to be responsible for taking care of me, I didn't think she should worry about chasing him down for money to feed and clothe me. That was the first and only time we talked about it. It stands out in my mind as one of my first lessons about the value of money, not just in the monetary sense but in its ability to provide comfort and stability.

Grandma handed over the reins for me to handle my own money very early. I was responsible for buying school clothes and other necessities, and looking back at myself then, I actually managed it pretty well. I was proud that she trusted me and I didn't take that lightly. Saving money was important to me because I was never sure when I was going to get it and where it was going to come from; I was protective of it—so much so that I opened a bank account when I was 10. Girls that age are quick to spend their allowances and monetary gifts on things they'll be tired of by the next year. Not me. I liked seeing the balance in my account grow. It empowered me, and because I'd learned that having money equaled having security, I felt safer knowing it was in there, especially since I'd always felt like I had to take care of myself. I wish I had known about stocks at the time because I probably could've paid for college when the time came, but there was no discussion about things like that. I didn't learn about buying stocks and the power of compounding until later in life.

The emotional roots of money

Money is an emotional trigger for many of us, either because of our own experiences with it or because of the way we watched our families relate to it when we were young. When I was growing up, the only times I ever saw my grandmother cry were connected to times when she was experiencing a money crisis. Don't get me wrong: She was a loving woman and expressed affection openly. She was emotive. She just didn't get visibly sad or upset often except when financial challenges were weighing on her and she had to try to figure out how to make them work. Those moments would overwhelm her. That's when I knew she was at a difficult point financially.

I think I was conscious of not wanting to add to her burden and I was always mature for my age. Because I had a more grown-up demeanor, I always had a job. I've been working since I was in elementary school. My neighbor, who was also my babysitter, had us working in tobacco fields. When I was a little older, I babysat and participated in summer job programs. I didn't mind working. A strong work ethic is inborn in me. My family may not have had a lot of money, but they worked hard for what they had and I inherited that trait from them. By the time I graduated from high school, I was ready to go off on my own. I've been completely independent since I was 19, but I've been working my whole life. I can't lie: Sometimes I'm exhausted. But it all came together—the way I was raised, my predisposition to be a saver, the lessons I've learned by trial and error—to push me into the field

I'm in and help other women build valuable investment portfolios.

I'm sure my grandmother didn't realize it at the time, but she helped me become a strong decision-maker. Years after she invited me to make a choice that affected our united future, I became a financial planner. I didn't set out to become one. It wasn't a childhood dream. It was an alignment of all of the things I've experienced and the skills I've been naturally blessed with.

I'm now a wife, mother, business owner, and speaker. Like you, I've got a lot going on most of the time. When I was young and naïve, I thought I could conquer the world, achieve anything, and transition my dreams into real-life successes. I'm a little older—and, I hope, a lot wiser—but I still believe those things, not only for myself, but for the women I work with and count among my clients. One of the things I'd hope to achieve as a superwoman in my own right is empowering my community. My purpose is to educate women about economic and financial empowerment. When I made this my career, I wasn't sure how I was going to do what I wanted to do. As I gained experience and clarified my professional vision, it came together. Now I talk to women about their feelings *and* their finances—remember I said that money matters are often tied to our emotions?—and discuss in detail where they envision themselves financially. I'm often saddened by their answers.

For example, I spoke to a woman who wanted to divorce her husband but couldn't because of her financial dependence on him, as well as the responsibilities they'd assumed together when her salary was higher than his and she was the primary breadwinner. She was forced to rebuild her career because of a job loss during a time when she had kids in college. Then there was the woman who couldn't afford to retire because she didn't have enough money saved; she'd created debt for herself when she refinanced her home to support her husband's business ventures. As a result, she hadn't accumulated enough to maintain her current lifestyle in retirement. Last, there was the woman who immigrated to the United States from Germany and married a former soldier who couldn't save a penny. She tried setting up a bank account for savings but learned after checking the account that the money was gone. If her husband knew there was money in the bank, he couldn't let it sit there and grow; he had to think of something to spend it on. So in order to save money, she had to literally hide it in places around the house like her undergarment drawer, a coffee can, or a cookie jar, places where he wouldn't look. She eventually accumulated more than $50,000, and when her husband died she invested it for her future. These encounters have deepened my resolve to help women in difficult situations. It's my duty to support them as they move past misguided decisions toward a better financial future.

I still see a critical need for financial education to help women make the best decisions for their families, their current lives, and their futures. So many of us remain silent when it comes to our finances and decisions that ultimately determine our financial destinies. There are two things I want you to remember about your finances: First, they are a key component to your success and stability; second, they can influence your mental and physical health. I know you want to do big, amazing things and check off big, amazing accomplishments. Your finances are your foundation to make that happen.

CHAPTER 2

Watch Out for Those Slingbacks: Money Mishaps to Avoid

*H*ave you ever purchased a pair of shoes that looked perfect for an outfit you had at home? You knew they would be the icing on the cake for the look you were trying to achieve. You were all ready to show off your stylish ensemble with that perfect pair of heels, and you headed off to your special event. After only an hour, your feet were swollen and numb because those "perfect" shoes just didn't fit properly— and you regretted the day you bought them. That can be the case with your finances. You look good from all angles but when you pull back the layers of who you are personally and what your money is doing, there's a mismatch.

When I talk to women about their finances, I'm disheartened by how much guidance is needed among executive and professional women. Financial education is crucial for women to make the best decisions—decisions that affect their families, their lives, and their futures. So many women remain silent when it comes to their finances and the choices that ultimately determine their financial destiny.

I read a report by CNN Money[2] that estimated one in eight American workers will never retire. *Never.* What's happening? Why aren't we more financially sound than our parents and grandparents? I believe that somewhere in our past, the focus shifted to immediate satisfaction and gratification versus some level of sacrifice in order to have a better future.

I've spent the past 13 years counseling smart and successful women about their finances, and I've noticed a pattern. There are mistakes those same smart, successful women regularly make when it comes to managing their money. Here are some common money missteps even the most savvy women make.

They wait for Prince Charming. You know the formula for fairy tales: A man rides in, bravely saves the damsel in distress, and they live happily ever after. Nowhere in the

---

[2] (One in 8 workers will never retire, 2013)

story is the damsel obligated to balance her checking account and pick an investment vehicle.

Once they're in a comfortable, long-term relationship, some women don't want to be involved in the financial affairs. They've been socialized to believe that a man should handle the income that flows into a household, so they wait for the man of their dreams to slay all their financial dragons. They assume he knows what he's doing, happily turn over the paperwork, and let him take the lead. That frees them up to focus on their families and careers and all the related duties.

In every relationship, you have to work out who takes the lead in each area of responsibility. That may mean your partner handles the money, but you should always stay involved and informed. If, God forbid, something happens to him, or your relationship ends, you shouldn't be left clueless.

They're at odds with their mate about money. On the other side of the Prince Charming scenario, some women have great difficulty sharing any kind of control with their partner. That's just as much of a mistake as giving it all up. Not only do you need to work jointly with your spouse, you should work toward the same goals and agree on how you're going to get there. He might be completely aggressive while you're not. You may be more willing to take risks than he is. Your investments should be decided jointly, including your 401(k). Financial decisions may be made in either of your names, but they affect the entire family.

They accumulate things, not assets. It's easy to unconsciously fall into the trap of keeping up with an image or a certain lifestyle, especially in the age of social media; we like to share what we're doing and reveal the finer points of our lives. We start buying things that represent the trappings of success rather than investing the money we use to buy those trappings.

I like nice things. I clearly come from kings and queens. I must have. Because when I go into a store, I intuitively pick out the most expensive item. A hard-working woman should enjoy the benefits of her labor; that's what life is about, creating memorable experiences. But be careful of mindless shopping and spending because it provides only a temporary gratification that needs to be balanced with maximizing the accumulation of assets that can appreciate in value. Rather than buying more stuff—because, as much as I believe in them, you really only need but so many pairs of shoes—set up a Roth or traditional IRA, or increase your contribution to your 401(k).

They wait too long to get started. I wish I had known how to invest when I was in high school. I knew to save but knew nothing about investing. It's important to let our teenagers know they can open investment accounts or IRAs when they start their summer jobs, and that as long as they don't go over the annual maximum contribution of $5,500, they can use that money to purchase a mutual fund, exchange traded funds (ETFs), or individual stocks. Although you may not have saved as a teen, it's a good life lesson to teach your daughter now, so she can take advantage of what you've learned. With guidance from your planner or an advisor, help your daughters pick the stocks they like. The market is made up of a pool of individual companies. Instead of buying another pair of boots, sandals, or pumps, buy stock in *the company that makes* the boots, sandals, or pumps. Do the same with video games, handbags, even television networks that air shows your children enjoy. You're helping them start taking their financial futures seriously and building a powerful legacy of financial wisdom.

Imagine what your investments would look like now if you'd started when you were 16. The earlier you start, the

Growth of savings accounts

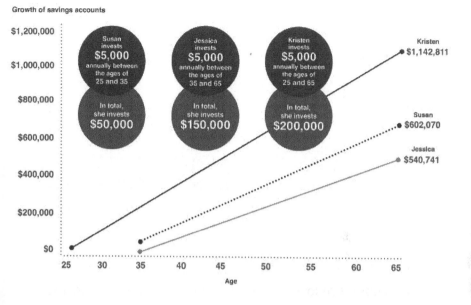

This example is for illustrative purposes only and reflects an annual rate of return of 7%. (Source: J.P. Morgan Asset Management)

more you'll be able to accumulate. A few years can make the difference between having $200,000, which is good, and banking $1 million, which is fantastic. The younger you are when you start, the more risk you can take. If you have 30 years to invest, there's no reason to be conservative. Spreading that risk around realizes greater returns. This is why asset allocation is important.

They don't invest enough of their salary. Investing a substantial percentage of your salary for retirement is just as important as starting early. Some women only contribute the percentage that is matched by their employers. For instance, if your company matches 5% of your salary and you earn $100,000 a year, you put aside $5,000. Your employer's match increases it to $10,000, but is that really enough? With a 401(k) you can contribute up to $18,000 of pretax income for 2015, bringing your annual contributions, with the company's match, to $23,000. If you are over 50, you can put in additional catch-up contributions of $6,000, for a total of $29,000. That grows your nest egg twice as quickly and you likely won't notice the difference in your paycheck. Your retirement savings should even be a major consideration when you negotiate your salary. Ask for a percentage that allows you to maximize your contributions.

They're too conservative with their investments. According to a report by Fidelity[3] on women investors, conservative investing could be the result of a lack of experience, a lack of knowledge, or just a lack of confidence. In any case, you can't afford to be too conservative; women tend to live longer than men, and as a result they incur more expenses in later years, from basic neces-

[3] (Fidelity Viewpoints, Women Investors: Four Tips, May 22, 2014)

sities to healthcare costs. The Great Recession of 2008 has left a mark on our consciousness that causes us to fear losing what we've accumulated. It's painful to open your investment or retirement statement and see your balance going down instead of up. But being conservative can slow the rate at which your money compounds, and you may not have what you need when you retire. You may have to work longer than you want to, or you may not be able to enjoy your life they way you want to because of drastic decisions you are forced to make about your livelihood. That's why you have to evaluate your investment decisions from other vantage points, measuring the risk versus reward and taking all these factors into account, not just your fear of losing money.

They act on emotion. I know this is a common myth about women, but it's not exclusive to us. Both genders are prone to making financial decisions based on their feelings, not facts. (Ever seen a smug, middle-aged man in a sports car he can't afford?) It's not a smart move for anyone to make, though, especially a woman. Life expectancy for women is getting longer, so decisions that impede our ability to make contributions to our portfolio can affect when we retire and what we are able to do throughout retirement.

What's worse, the financial news media is designed to scare you and provoke you to react. When you notice that you are responding to a fear resulting from a personal life event or something brought on by current events, it's a good idea to get a professional opinion before making a rash decision. Ask a credible advisor to listen to your concerns and give you an informed viewpoint.

They put everyone else first. I think many of us are built with a selfless gene. We want to take care of our loved ones, and we often do so to our own detriment. For instance, we want to send our kids to good colleges, and many of us mortgage our own futures unnecessarily. If you withdraw from your retirement to pay for your children's tuition, you have fewer years to earn that money back. Sometimes helping your kids is finding a happy medium. Please do not jeopardize your own retirement for your children's education. There's nothing wrong with them taking out a loan. After all, there's no guarantee that they will be able to take care of you if you reach retirement age and are out of money.

They don't get insurance. If you get sick or hurt, you can't work. If you can't work, you can't make money. If you can't make money, you can't build wealth. Because of the potentially devastating result of such a domino effect, you should have disability insurance. If it's offered at your job, start there—it's usually less expensive, even though benefits are taxed if you need to use them and cover up to a set percentage of your salary, generally 60%. Purchasing a policy in addition to the one at your job has tax perks and may provide better coverage, such as shorter elimination periods (the length of time before you begin receiving payments) and a higher monthly payment for a longer period of time.

Long-term-care insurance is a good idea at any age, but you should seriously look at it when you get into your mid-to-late 40s. Your age can significantly affect the cost of a policy. Generally, the younger you are, the lower the premium. If you experience a debilitating illness, you don't have to spend your savings or create a financial burden for your family. Worse than that, if you're left to the public system, you may have limited choices as to where you are placed if you have extended healthcare needs. Many people don't realize that Medicare covers only a certain number of days limited to a specific monetary amount. When woman uses her Medicare insurance during the first 20 days, she pays nothing; for days 21–100, she pays a coinsurance of $157.50 per day; and beginning on day 101, she is responsible for *all* costs.[4]

[4] (Medicare.gov, n.d.)

I learned this when my mother had a stroke and needed to go to a rehabilitation facility in Virginia. Placement was based on availability and could have resulted in her being placed anywhere in the state. Fortunately she was placed in a nearby facility, but learning about her options was overwhelming. I gained an understanding of how confusing the Medicare system can be, especially when you are juggling a lot of medical decisions at once.

Once you have children, life insurance becomes a necessity. It's not the sexiest purchase you'll ever make, but not having it can negatively affect your livelihood. A friend learned that she had breast cancer when she turned 40. With that type of illness, getting life insurance outside of your job will be almost impossible. You have to be in remission for at least five years.

They don't seek advice soon enough. Women not making the best choices for their financial futures don't seek their ounce of prevention and end up stuck with the pound of cure. Too many times, I get a call *after* a costly mistake has been made, rather than before. You wouldn't sue someone without consulting a lawyer (at least I hope not). So when you're confronting an important financial decision, it helps to talk through issues with someone who has expertise in that area—just as you rely on your girlfriends to bounce ideas off and ask for guidance for personal decisions. It's like a company using its board of directors for insight and advice on decisions that impact its direction; they may have ideas that you never thought about. Advisors encounter different financial scenarios every day. We're problem-solvers. A smart woman seeks the insight of a Certified Financial Planner who best suits her personality and personal investment style.

You may be wondering how much it costs. As I've shared, working with a good financial planner can literally change your life. That's why it's important to understand the fee structures, so you can determine which one best suits you. Here are four ways advisors can get paid: commission, commission and fee, salary plus bonuses, and fee-only.

Commission only. This is when advisors receive only commissions for selling financial services products.

Commission and fees. Another term commonly used is fee-based. Commission-and-fee advisors may receive a fee for developing a financial plan for you and then receive commissions when they sell you insurance and investment products recommended in your financial plan.

Salary plus bonuses. Discount brokerage firms and banks compensate their employees with a base salary plus incentive pay for bringing in new clients and recommending or selling certain products and services.

Fee only. Fee-only financial advisors provide advice or ongoing management. Certified Financial Planners generally fall within this category but can utilize the other fee structures as well. They're typically self-employed Registered Investment Advisors (RIA) or employees of this type of firm. Fee-only financial advisors have no financial stake in the recommendations they give you. They may charge in three ways: hourly fee, flat fee, and/or retainer fee.

Hourly fee. You pay for all the time that the financial advisor works on your case or spends with you. Multiply the time spent by the advisor's hourly charge, and that's how much your fee is. Always find out the expected cost and the maximum cost before you begin working with an advisor who charges by the hour. This may be best for:

- People who need specific advice about one or a few financial topics.

- Do-it-yourselfers who just want a professional's opinion.

- People who want to do as much as possible to save money but want expert analysis and direction.

Flat fee. You pay a flat (one-time) fee for specific services. Flat-fee pricing may be an alternative for people who need specific advice or services.

Retainer fee. A retainer fee is often calculated based on a percentage of assets the advisor manages, your net worth or income, or a mixture of the two; or by estimating the amount of time required and the complexity of the services promised. A retainer fee may be good for people who want ongoing assistance managing their financial affairs.

Moment of truth: Did you see yourself in any of those scenarios? There's no need to be ashamed or embarrassed if you did. Many smart and successful women find themselves in these situations because there are old habits to break and new behaviors to incorporate. We have to retrain ourselves to operate from a more informed place when it comes to our finances. The good news? Once you recognize the mistakes, you've taken the first step to correcting them.

My grandmother was a huge influence in my life, and that influence is one reason why my financial choices are so important to me. For most of the time I lived with her, she was the primary breadwinner. I saw how hard it was bearing that burden alone. It left a major imprint on my life and money habits. I watched my grandmother struggle with her finances and a lack of knowledge regarding her options, and I see that with many of my clients. I've been told on many occasions, "I wish I had met you when I was younger." Women tell me they could have avoided taking on too much consumer debt, started investing sooner toward their retirements, or opted not to cash out of a 401(k) after leaving a job. Because of my grandmother, when I hear these statements I feel it's important to be empathetic. When you lack knowledge and guidance, you make mistakes. It's important to acknowledge and learn from them, but I encourage focusing your efforts on moving past them. That's how you grow.

Wall Street is your runway

When I read fashion blogs and magazines—I *have* to

keep up with who's wearing what on their feet—I often wonder if women have ownership in the items they wear beyond just having paid for them in the store. Many ladies go to Neiman Marcus (stock symbol: NMG), Bloomingdale's (M), and Nordstrom (JWN) to shop for their fabulously stylish ensembles. Frugal gals who like to find a good deal may go to Tanger Outlets (SKT), Marshalls, and T.J. Maxx (both TJX). Since I understand the euphoria that many of us get from shopping, why not own the brands you love so much in a different way? Purchase their stock.

I'm not advocating going out and making a stock purchase just because you like the store. That would be impulsive. You have to do your research. Start by reviewing the corporate information available on the company's website. Nordstrom's investor relations page, for example, has the company's current stock price, earnings releases, performance summaries, annual report, annual (10-K) and quarterly (10-Q) financial statements, proxy statement, and proxy voting results, all required by the U.S. Securities and Exchange Commission. This information tells you many things about the company, including how it's performing financially, what the plans are for future growth, what the business lines are within the company, and who represents their management team and board of directors.

Specifically, the annual report on Form 10-K provides a comprehensive overview of the company's business and financial condition and includes audited financial statements. A company's proxy statement details pertinent information about the board of directors. Knowing all this allows an investor to make an informed decision about voting for the board to represent her interest. That's why it's important to vote your proxy after you purchase stock. Investor advocacy starts with your vote.

The board of directors is responsible for protecting the company's assets; ensuring the company provides investors a reasonable return; selecting and approving the CEO's compensation; evaluating dividend payouts, stock splits, and share repurchases; and approving or disapproving mergers and acquisitions. Some of you may be on corporate boards and understand your responsibility to shareholders.

From the website, you should be able to learn about the overall mission and how it's exhibited within the internal workings of the company. Of course, there are many other sites where you can find out more about the fiscal side of the stores and labels you love. That way you can start to understand if a company you support as a shopper is really worth your money as an investor. It's one way of turning your fashion proclivities into a financial asset.

There are also investments to be made in jewelry. My husband and I had friends over one evening, and during the course of conversation they mentioned that they'd just celebrated their 10-year anniversary. My friend's gift to his wife was an upgrade of the engagement ring he'd bought when he proposed to her. When they exchanged the starter diamond for a new and improved version, they were surprised that it had appreciated so much in the last decade.

We know how important that ring is when he gets down on one knee to pop the question, so when we sense that he may be thinking about it, we start giving him hints—leaving out articles detailing the four C's (carat, color, clarity and cut) of diamonds, casually window shopping at jewelry stores when we walk through the mall—all so he will select *the* perfect ring. Of course, the ring will be a symbol of your love and commitment, and it will have great sentimental value to you, but it can also have considerable monetary value and be a significant addition to your portfolio.

If you're a fan of "Sex and the City," you may remember the episode in which Charlotte gave Carrie her Tiffany engagement ring as a loan so Carrie could put a down payment on an apartment. That gesture showed how much Charlotte valued their friendship, but it also demonstrated the price tag that jewelry can have. (If that was for the entire down payment, $30,000 isn't even as expensive as a Tiffany ring can get!)[5]

The Rapaport Group, established in 1976, operates a diamond-pricing service. The company recommends an initial investment be in round diamonds, 1.01 to 1.49 carats, D–H color, IF-VS2 clarity, excellent to very good cut. Rapaport specification is 2+ diamonds. These diamonds trade on a daily basis, their prices are well-known, and they're easy to purchase and sell. If you don't know what this means, find out before you make an investment.

Here are a few other tips: Always get your diamond authenticated by the Gemological Institute of America (GIA), the primary diamond-grading authority, and confirmed by a personal diamond expert. A diamond is not worth having if you can't determine its value. With diamonds, you need to look at price, transparency, quality

[5] (Find Your Perfect Engagement Ring, n.d.)

assurance, transaction costs, and liquidity. Stay away from large, expensive (spectacular) diamonds. They may appreciate in value, but they're difficult to sell because each diamond has unique qualities and features, thereby making it difficult to compare. As an investor, you may find it hard to determine if you are receiving the true value of a diamond. For any investment, the value is driven by supply and demand and the amount someone is willing to pay for it. That's the downside to this type of investment, so it may not be the best way to grow your nest egg. You can't buy too many pairs of Jimmy Choos in your retirement if you can't make your assets liquid when you want to. But the smaller carats are something to think about when looking for diversification beyond stocks and bonds. Just proceed with caution.

As I'm writing this, there are no mutual funds or ETFs that invest exclusively in diamonds. The Rapaport Group tracks diamond prices globally and works directly with individuals with a minimum of $100,000 to invest. So the next time he asks for gift ideas for your special anniversary, a promotion, or a new addition to the family, consider adding to your diamond collection. Based on this information, I will be reappraising my engagement ring and wedding band.

From my experience, investing in various instruments has been a powerful way to multiply the growth in my personal retirement savings and that of my husband. Even though I might be more aggressive than most women, I still believe in diversification. Because of the recent bull market and the fact that my husband and I stayed invested during the recession, we have seen our portfolio double in value. That's why I feel it is important to understand the Rule of 72, which approximates how long it will take for your portfolio to double in value: Given a specific rate of return, and dividing this rate into 72, investors can determine roughly how many years it will take for their initial investment to double. This rule can help you to evaluate one element of risk versus reward: return on investment. So if your portfolio of $200,000 earns an annualized return of 10% (averages 10% annually), it will take about 7.2 years for your money to double to $400,000. With the continual growth of our portfolio through increased contributions and compounding due to investment return, we anticipate reaching our retirement goals. That's why I reiterate that you should not allow missteps to hinder you from accumulating your wealth goals.

CHAPTER 3

Perfect Like a Pair of Peep-Toes: Money + Love

*T*here are some women who just have to have a new pair of shoes to match every outfit in their wardrobes. You walk in their closets and you see the evidence of their spending habits, shoes from the ceiling to the floor occupying quite a bit of square footage. If you are one of these women, it may cause many arguments between you and your spouse, probably because he just doesn't understand the need for all those shoes and why you spend so much money on them. To him it's a complete waste. So you hide your purchases, avoid financial discussions, and end up arguing over them. You may even feel guilt for spending money that could be used somewhere else in the household. If you can afford it, great; but if you can't, is your spending on shoes hiding unresolved issues or an unhealthy relationship you have with money? Learning about your money triggers can help.

It's been said by just about every expert in the financial industry and I'll reiterate it: If you can't comfortably and amicably discuss money with your partner, you're heading for relationship—and possibly financial—disaster. It's normal for couples to fight over their finances, but that doesn't mean it's healthy. Watch a few episodes of "Divorce Court" and keep track of how many times one spouse complains about the other's out-of-control spending habits or tight-fisted saving. If you're not experiencing that kind of drama in your own relationship, take a moment to be thankful. According to a survey published by Money magazine[6], 70% of couples argue more about money than about household chores, sex, snoring, spending time together, and what's for dinner. Those fights center around debt, household budgeting, and the always controversial frivolous purchases (symbolized in the article by—what else?—a picture of shoes).

Money represents many things in the context of a partnership or marriage, even in the early dating stage: power, status, security, communication, affection, success. But without a unified approach, it also contributes to arguments, posturing, dishonesty, alienation, secrecy, and

[6] (Love and Money - By the Numbers, 2014)

frustration. That negativity can seep into other parts of your relationship, but it's avoidable and just not worth it. When you're single, you need a strategy for building savings, making wise spending decisions, accumulating wealth, and protecting your assets. So when you factor another person into the financial equation, the need for a strategy doubles. Getting to know a person—*really* getting to know them—is understanding early his relationship with money. It's not usually an easy or comfortable conversation to have, but there are clues that you can look for to ease the introduction of the topic.

When I met the man who would become my husband, Chris, I was 29 years old. There were certain things that impressed me about him: He was an active member of an investment club, so I knew he valued investing for the future. He is very thorough about tracking his finances; even now he updates Quicken with all our family purchases, savings, and investments. He's extremely conscientious when making purchases; he does research and makes comparisons before coming to a final decision to buy. He lived within his means. He never spent money on things he couldn't afford. He saved regularly, so if there was something he needed, he planned and set money aside for the purchase. He maxed out his retirement savings each year. He shared with me that this was advice given to him from his father when he started working. I admired his money-management skills because they aligned with mine.

The real difference between men and women

It wasn't love at first sight with Chris, but it was a strong attraction, at least on my part. I thought he was cute, intelligent, and well-mannered. He impressed me so much, it was easy to begin imagining what life with him would be like. Because I knew finances are a major reason for disagreements with couples, I paid close attention to his skills around money to determine if we would be financially compatible.

We dated for five years, so I learned a lot about his money habits and he learned about mine. One of the many compliments he gives me is that he finds no need to question me about my spending because he trusts me to make good money decisions. I don't need to hide my purchases from him.

After 10 years of marriage, I've learned that he and I have different experiences with money. We both are savers and were good at managing our individual finances. Now we use our different approaches to manage our household.

amazon Gift Receipt

Send a Thank You Note

You can learn more about your gift or start a return here too

Scan using the Amazon app or visit
https://a.co/d/1vogxa6

Finance 'n Stilettos

Order ID: 114-0316021-1353027   Ordered on September 6, 2022

A gift for you

Enclosed is your Zip Book. When finished, please return the item and note to the desk of any Sacramento Public Library. From Sacramento Public Library Zip Book

amazon.com

SXBFMVKGQM

Order of September 6, 2022

Qty.   Item

---

1   **Finance 'n Stilettos**
       Harris CFP®, Zaneilia --- Paperback
       1457541572
       1457541572 9781457541575

Return or replace your item
Visit Amazon.com/returns

0/XBFMVKGQM/-1 of 1-//KILN-KTPA-A-CART/next-1dc/0/0907-09:00/0906-19:54   SmartPa

My strengths are with our family's overall investment and money strategy, whereas he's extremely thorough and a computer geek, so he manages our monthly finances and keeps them up-to-date electronically. Talking has been key to us working well together.

Last year I celebrated my birthday on a date night with Chris and another couple. Over the course of dinner, we got on the subject of women and finances. I shared how my goal is to engage and educate more women to participate in the finances of the home beyond just the household budget. My male friend, "the husband," asked me, "What makes you think men want their wives to be knowledgeable about finances?"

I was stunned. His wife is an educated, articulate, professional woman. I never thought such a question could have rolled off his tongue. As you can imagine, the conversation became quite "interesting" after that.

I wondered how many men felt the same way as my friend. Needless to say, even if they all do, my opinion is that women need to demand to be a part of the family's finances. *All of them.* Your outlook is a valuable part of the decision-making, and you may bring a new perspective to helping your family reach a financial goal. Your opinion matters, so don't disengage or allow yourself to be forced out. I said as much during the course of our dinner discussion.

Women have been socialized to worry about three things: finding a husband, marrying a husband, and keeping a husband, because not being alone is a critical component to having a happy life. (And everyone wants a happy life, right?) But the financial responsibilities that are part of an equal partnership are so often imbalanced, falling to men who may not be any better at balancing a checkbook or selecting a stock than the other duties they willingly turn over to their spouses. But because he's a male he's been conditioned to believe that this is his manly duty, and we've been conditioned early to believe that "math is hard" and "boys are better with numbers." Both genders carry those lessons into our marriages, and many women willingly relinquish the heavy financial lifting to our significant others.

As contradictory as it may sound, our families have also groomed most of us to be independent, at least on some level, and that needs to extend to our finances. There are three key things that should drive our financial relationships, even in the context of a romantic relationship.

Learn how to negotiate, negotiate, negotiate. It is a skill that will benefit you in innumerable ways. Shake off shyness and fear to get what you deserve. Ask for a raise at work to increase your take-home pay so you can tuck more away in savings. Call your loan and credit card companies to demand a lower interest rate. Review contracts with cell phone, cable, and internet service providers annually and inquire about renewal discounts. It takes practice but it's well worth the effort.

Pay yourself first. Always. This is a primary rule as a professional woman. Put your savings on autopilot. Create allotments from your paycheck that automatically go into accounts for emergencies, retirement, and your child(ren)'s education. Being financially stable means having a well-rounded portfolio of liquid and long-term assets that includes bonds, growth, value, small- and large-cap companies, and alternative options such as commodities or hedge strategies.

The benefit on the money side is having immediate funds in case of emergency or opportunity, whenever you need quick access. The benefit on the personal side is being in control of accumulating savings, which leads to confidence, which leads to empowered decisions.

DOMESTIC EQUITY
- Large Value
- Large Blend
- Mid Cap Blend
- Mid Gap Growth
- Small Value
- Small Blend
- Small Growth

FOREIGN EQUITY
- Large Cap
- Small Cap
- Emerging Markets
- Frontier

ALTERNATIVE INVESTMENTS
- Convertibles
- Hedged Equity
- Private Equity
- Commodities
- Currencies
- Hedged Equity
- Global Real Estate

FIXED INCOME
- Tips
- Global
- High Yield
- Stable Value
- Short Bend
- Intermediate Bond

Protect what you have. Make sure you have the appropriate health, disability, life, and long-term-care insurance coverage so you won't have to worry about money at a time when you are in great distress.

Hopefully, you will stay in blissful, happy love for the rest of your life. Love is a beautiful thing and I'm glad that I have an opportunity to experience it. The reality of relationships—all relationships—is that there will be challenges, ups, downs, shocks, and surprises. We have to think about and be prepared for our futures with or without significant others. I would do women, especially single women, an injustice if I don't share some reality.

Have a genuine discussion about money with your boo or spouse. It's not romantic pillow talk, but neither is arguing over a bill or an unplanned splurge. Schedule a time to discuss it so you can stay aligned with one another in this area and reduce the potential for frustration.

The finances of going from miss to missus

From a business perspective, the wedding season is a time for professionals to cash in on love. In 2014, the average American wedding cost was close to $31,000—$31,218 to be exact—the highest ever, according to The Knot.[7] Only 20% of engaged couples tightened their budgets because of a still-recovering economy. It was reported that one in eight couples spent more than $40,000 on their big day, and almost one in four had no budget at all. A budget-less wedding? Wow, money can't buy love but it sure can buy a big celebration.

When Chris and I planned our wedding, I kept a close eye on the budget, limiting our outlay to approximately $20,000. Thanks to my persistence, we even received a $1,000 refund from the reception venue. That money went straight into our savings account.

[7] (The Knot, The #1 Wedding Site, Releases 2014 Real Weddings Study Statistics, 2015)

I know this is an exciting time, with all the planning details from the flowers, bridesmaids' dresses, and cake selections to the highly anticipated wedding gown. It's a joyous time in your life. And as a newlywed, you're in wedding bliss. You're sharing your life with the one you love and it can be hard to imagine that anything disappointing would or could happen to disrupt your happiness. Talk about your plans as a couple beyond that day. Think about what you want to achieve. This should open the door to an honest discussion about your hopes and dreams as a family. Understanding your overall vision helps you set specific goals and estimate the costs to achieve them.

With this begins your first test as a newlywed: learning the art of compromise. Be frank about the vision you desire for your family and develop an approach to achieving it together. The next major event after the wedding for most couples is having children. According to a report from the Department of Agriculture, it will cost $241,080 for a middle-income couple to raise a child to age 18. This shows how much of an investment children are financially, but there's also an emotional, psychological, mental, and spiritual investment. I can attest to that, and if you're a mother, you probably can, too.

When I was pregnant with my daughter, Madison, it was amazing how my perspective on life changed. I contemplated whether I should go back to work or stay home for the first year. Honestly, I couldn't believe I was thinking about being a stay-at-home mom. Having a baby does something to you. Raising children is a lifelong commitment with a lot of sacrifices. Once they come along, will both you and your spouse remain in the workforce? When evaluating your family's budget, can you afford to lose an income? If your family's goal is for one parent to stay at home, discuss which of you will do it and for how long. Since cost is one of the major considerations, here are five things to think about as you draft up your plan:

1. Start living on one income and save the other. Then it won't be a big adjustment when the first child joins the family and one of you stays home.

2. Set a goal to maximize your family's retirement savings. Build your household budget with the savings contributions included. The sooner you begin, the longer the money will be able to work for you.

3. Consider working part-time. This will help you keep one foot in the workforce and maintain your professional skills.

4. Ensure the adjusted household budget allows for contribution to a spousal IRA.

5. Establish a network and professional relationships with other parents by volunteering at your child's school. This could lead to future job opportunities.

Love and loss

When I tell people what I do, the conversation often turns to a lot of personal reflection on their part and a lot of compassionate listening on mine. A woman I'd just met told me she handles the day-to-day budget for food, clothing, and other family necessities in her household, and her husband takes care of the long-term aspects of their finances. One winter, a major snowstorm hit her area, causing several serious accidents. Her husband was returning home from out of town, and she was nervous about him being on the road. During this time she had a revelation: She didn't know what she would do if something happened to him.

She asked herself, "Will I know how to handle everything around our finances beyond what I currently do?" She couldn't answer her own question with certainty, and I certainly couldn't answer it for her. It's a frightening situation to be in, even theoretically, yet many women find themselves in it, especially if they've recently gone through a divorce or the death of a spouse.

The loss of a spouse is devastating, overwhelming some individuals to the point where they completely shut down because not only is the death emotional, money is emotional too. Others become so busy that they focus only on what needs to get done. It's a somber topic, but it needs contemplation and preparation just like any other area of your finances.

The first thing to think about: Don't rush to make any major decisions. It's an emotionally devastating time, particularly in the first several days. Take care of your mental, emotional, and spiritual self before you address the issues around money. When you're ready, use this spouse survivor checklist to help guide and ease you through the process:

Locate your family's important papers. This would include your trust, will, insurance policies, bank statements, pension statements, 401(k) documentation, and IRAs. Gather as much as possible and continue to do so for the next few weeks.

Be prepared for some red tape. Certain jointly held assets, such as safe deposit boxes and checking accounts, may be frozen as soon as your banking institution becomes aware that one of the owners has died. Although those assets are intended to pass to the surviving spouse when the normal probate process is complete, actual possession may be delayed pending a court-ordered release. This may depend on proof of inheritance or estate-tax documents that show other assets adequate to pay potential estate or inheritance tax.

Request copies of the death certificate. Contact your state's office of vital statistics for multiple copies of the official certificate (there may be a fee). You'll need to submit one to the deceased's employer, life insurance companies, and creditors.

Have copies of your spouse's birth certificate and Social Security card, as well as your marriage license. You will need to include additional proof of life to various entities, such as financial institutions, federal and state governments, courts, and former employer(s) to obtain information and receive benefits.

Notify your attorney. Make an appointment to review your spouse's will and discuss state and federal death taxes that may be payable.

Contact life or accident insurers. Be sure to provide the deceased's name, date of death, and Social Security number and a copy of the death certificate.

Call your spouse's former employer. Find out about his retirement, pension, and life insurance benefits. You'll need to provide his name, date of death, and Social Security number and a copy of the death certificate.

Change necessary ownership. There may be more depending on your assets, but address the following in particular:

- stocks
- vehicles
- bonds
- investments
- properties
- bank and credit accounts
- safe deposit boxes
- estate planning documents (i.e., will and trust)

For more helpful information, read the book "Moving Forward on Your Own" by Kathleen M. Rehl.

Can I be honest about us for a moment? We can't let love make us soft. Goals are still just as important when you are part of a couple as they are when you are single. Be clear about where you want to be, do your research, and talk to a professional. Have difficult conversations with your spouse or significant other to clarify expectations and objectives. This can be easier with the counsel of your financial planner. Having a neutral party can help the conversation move toward specific goals. And as you do your own research and discuss it with your partner, learn what information pertains specifically to you and what information you should discard because it's irrelevant to where you're trying to go and what you're financially trying to do for your family.

A few years ago, I read an article in the Wall Street Journal about the rise in divorce among baby boomers. More couples are deciding that, since the kids are older, they have grown apart and no longer want to remain married. Within my family and among some of my friends, I've seen the effects of it. I feel divorce can be just as devastating as a death, both emotionally and financially. It's the death of a relationship, and you can experience the same stages of grief. That's why it's important to hire a team of advisors (divorce attorney, arbitrator, financial advisor, and therapist) to help guide you through the process objectively.

Some key points to consider are establishing a budget based on your life (single, possibly with kids) and estimating your current cash flow and expenses. Start collecting all joint debt, bank and investment accounts, insurance policies, and other marital assets. And don't forget about any IRA, 401(k), 403(b), or pension accounts. If you can, gather statements from when you first got married. This will provide a timeline of premarital and marital assets. Share copies of this information with your attorney and financial planner. You should meet with them together so you can obtain different perspectives prior to finalizing any major decisions. Going through a divorce can be adversarial, agonizing, and exhausting, so meet with your therapist to help you process your emotions.

I cannot emphasize enough the importance of knowing about your family's finances. One thing about life is that it's full of changes. Some we welcome and some we wish we'd never experience. Through it all, it presents an opportunity to learn and grow. Though I haven't experienced divorce personally, I have witnessed its effects on some women in my life, so don't allow emotions to drive decisions that will affect the rest of your life. I did this when my grandmother asked about my dad paying child support. My pride took over and we made a completely irrational decision that changed my life. I hope I can help you learn from our mistake.

CHAPTER 4

Being Mary Janes: The Intersection of Wealth and Your Financial Future

I'm not much of a TV person but I was home one evening, flipping through an endless number of cable channels airing nothing good, when I came across "Chris Rock: Never Scared."[8] I like a good laugh and he's a funny guy, so I stopped to watch. One part in particular caught my attention. He joked about the differences between being rich and being wealthy:

> *Shaq is rich. The [man] that signs his check is wealthy ... If Bill Gates woke up tomorrow with Oprah's money, he'd jump out a ... window ... I'm not talking about rich, I'm talking about ... wealth.*

[8] (Rock, 2004)

Wealth is passed down from generation to generation. You can't get rid of wealth. Rich ... you can lose with a crazy summer and a drug habit. Rick James was rich. One minute you're singing "Super Freak," the next minute you're doing Old Navy commercials.

That made me chuckle, but it also got me thinking about what it means to be rich versus wealthy as it relates to financial planning. When I think of being "rich," and the people who typically fit that category, I also wonder how long the money lasts and why "rich" doesn't always mean "wealthy," even though the two words are generally used interchangeably. In the previously mentioned episode of "Sex in the City," titled "Ring a Ding Ding," you may remember Carrie's apartment is being converted to a co-op and she doesn't have the money to purchase it without the help of her ex-boyfriend Mr. Big? Miranda points out to Carrie that she's wasted $40,000 on her shoe obsession but can't afford a place to live.[9] As I'm watching this, I'm thinking, how can this happen? It shows the major difference between having money and wearing it. That's why, in the financial world, being rich and wealthy are very different. They are in the rest of the world too, but we just don't notice it because so many of

[9] (Taylor, 2002)

us are trying to get to the level where we can be considered one or the other; we're not splitting hairs about the differences between the two.

Wealth is tangible and intangible. Wealthy people invest their money in assets that keep making them more money. They then use that advantage to create more advantage that translates to power, influence, and favor. Wealth is also generational legacy. When you make plans to leave a legacy that goes beyond your life, it has to transcend just passing assets to heirs. Wealth is about teaching your heirs your core values and history so they can expand on that work. It is about growing, building, and sharing for the future. Think of the Waltons with their chain of Wal-Mart stores, the Mars family for their candy empire, and the descendants of S.C. Johnson for cleaning products such as Pledge and Windex, which are raking in upwards of $25 billion nearly 130 years after the company was founded. They are heirs to a financial and business legacy left by someone generations ago and consistently top the Forbes list as some of America's most financially successful and culturally influential families.

Rich, on the other hand, is a first-generation accumulation of a large sum of cash. Rich is "new money." Lottery winners who hit it big, athletes who sign life-changing, multimillion dollar contracts, and recording artists who have a hit song or two (if they're lucky, three, four or more) are rich. There's nothing wrong with that. Everybody has to start somewhere, and if that happens because of hard work or tremendous luck or a combination of the two, it doesn't really matter. It's what the people on the receiving end of those windfalls choose to do with the funds that determines whether they'll become wealthy or stay rich (and for how long).

Love or hate Beyoncé musically, you can't help but be a fan of her business acumen. She has been quoted as saying, "I have a lot of property. I've invested my money and I don't have to make anymore because I'm set. I'm now able really to be free and just do things that make me happy." These statements are so powerful because they confirm that women can be smart with their finances. I truly appreciate a woman who is savvy about protecting her assets and diversifying her investments. She's living the financial dream of many woman: to be free from financial burdens, to just be happy. I know it's mine and my goal for other women as well.

Financial strategies for high-profile women

In my 20 years of experience I've met intelligent women guilty of making the occasional money misstep, even those who work in high-profile positions and are fortunate to have access to a slew of financial advisors and resources.

What's the key to bouncing back with grace and dignity? Don't beat yourself up. Simply learn from your mistakes and move on. Protect yourself from future missteps by learning from others' financial errors. You don't have to make every mistake yourself. Pay attention to what other people have learned through their own experiences and apply them to yourself. It's free wisdom. I'd like to see us moving down the path to greater wealth. It's one of the issues I discuss with my Savvy Women Investor Circle (SWIC) members: Let's make decisions that make us wealthy rather than just rich.

Be informed *before* **making a major decision or big transition.** Whether reevaluating your investments, taking out a large loan, making a major purchase, changing your marital status, negotiating salary, or even switching jobs, make sure you have all the facts. Speak with others who have successfully navigated their way through similar situations, interview professionals with expertise in your specific circumstances, and research, research, research.

Protect your legacy. You can never be too prepared. When "The View" cohost Sherri Shepherd filed for divorce from Lamar Sally, many questioned why she didn't seek custody of their then-unborn child being carried by a surrogate. But the issue had already been addressed in their prenuptial agreement, which stated that Sherri would receive full custody if they ever separated. (Whew!) On the other hand, because Whitney Houston hadn't revisited her estate plan before her untimely passing, her multimillion-dollar estate caused problems within her immediate family. After the premature death of her daughter, Bobbi Kristina, who had received an initial distribution of 10% from her mother's estimated $20 million estate as part of her inheritance, there was more publicity surrounding the division of Whitney's estate. That's why when you're establishing your estate documentation, you can't leave anything to chance. Hire an estate attorney to help you create the legacy you want to achieve, so you can control your estate beyond the grave. As your life changes, don't forget to update your documentation to ensure it addresses your current desires. If Whitney had created a trust, her finances could have been better protected from estate taxes and her personal information kept private. But her mistake was a reminder to the rest of us: Don't procrastinate completing all the components to make your estate plan executable at death according to your wishes.

Don't make a major decision when you're in distress. If you don't have to, don't take action until you absolutely know what steps you want to take, and again, learn from example. Perhaps one of the most famous divorce settlements in history was between Bob and Sheila Johnson, cofounders of BET. In 2000[10], Bob Johnson sold the network to Viacom for $3 billion. When the power couple's 33-year marriage ended and they divorced two years after the BET sale, citing "professional differences," Sheila walked away with $400 million in the settlement. In situations like that, it can be hard to know where loyalties lie among a couple's advisory team. That's why it's important to seek separate counsel and try to keep emotions at bay so you can respond from a position of strength. It saddens me that she didn't get half of their combined net worth, which is obviously $1.5 billion. If you're not sure what to do, take some time to think through your options. Don't make decisions out of haste.

[10] (Viacom pays $2.3B for BET , 2000)

Protect your net worth. When Shelly Sterling, former co-owner of the Los Angeles Clippers, sat down for a 2014 interview with Barbara Walters, she admitted that she was advised by her attorney and financial advisor not to divorce her estranged husband, Donald Sterling, because doing so would affect some of their financial arrangements. (Barbara has a way of getting people to tell all of their business, doesn't she?) The Sterlings live in California, a community property state, which means that if they divorce, she is entitled to receive half of all their marital assets. The details surrounding the advice she received are not public, but her advisers could have expected that by delaying a divorce, their combined net worth would increase, thereby giving her a larger amount to split between them once they did divorce. Initially, she was hoping he would transfer his half of the Clippers ownership to her, but he fought it despite Shelly agreeing to sell the team to former Microsoft CEO Steve Ballmer for $2 billion. Understand that this is only a portion of the amount due to Shelly for staying married. As she said—and a lot of women with significant assets echo her sentiments—her portion of the assets is part of her family's legacy. That's why having a good advisory team already in place is important to the overall protection of your assets.

Finally, be open to fresh ideas. As in any industry, the world of finance is constantly in flux. Being open to fresh ideas, new perspectives, and continual change will better prepare you for a stable and successful financial future.

CHAPTER 5

Balancing on Sky-High Platforms: Enter the Adventure of Investing

$\mathcal{A}$fter you reach a certain age and have achieved a certain level of financial security, you know you can splurge every now and again on a special pair of stilettoes, perhaps for an annual gala you attend to support a charity near and dear to your heart. You know shoes don't make the woman, but having the right pair for any event enhances your confidence because 1) you look elegant and classy, and 2) you can comfortably afford them. Why? Because you've made choices that align with your values and prioritized your saving and investing. Wow, what a wonderful mental place to be in.

I was talking to a friend about retirement and what that would look like for me. I envision a life where I am volunteering, traveling, and spending time with family and friends. I'm sure many of you have done pictured your life in your golden years. And yet I read an article, "Women Face a Host of Obstacles to Retirement," in USA Today several years ago that resonated with me and overwhelmed me with emotion. It still does. The story featured several women of retirement age living lives that I would venture to say they never expected. One woman had taken early retirement and had been working a part-time job for extra income. When the economy crashed, she, like a lot of people, lost her job and hadn't been able to find another. After several deaths in her family and shouldering the funeral expenses, she lost her home and was living in a YWCA. The second woman couldn't afford to retire. She was financially supporting a household comprising her grandchildren and her mother, who was suffering from Alzheimer's disease. Neither of those women was enjoying their retirement. It seemed they were just living through it.

Not long after that, I saw an Oprah interview with Paula Deen from 2012. I was so surprised to hear that despite the success she has enjoyed and the sizable "nest egg" she has amassed, she still has a recurring dream that she will end up penniless. At that moment I was reminded again of the overwhelming fear so many women have about their finances. Paula also shared how she hoped her success would leave a legacy so her children would not have to live a life without. (Of course, I'm paraphrasing, but that's the gist of it.) I believe at the end of the day, being financially secure is one of the most important things in the lives of women because it's how we care and provide for our families. Money doesn't translate to love, but the assurance that comes with it helps us express it.

According to Alexandra Penney, author of "The Bag Lady Papers: The Priceless Experience of Losing It All", many successful women have a fear of going broke and becoming homeless. In reports about women and finance, the sentiments are repeated over and over again: Am I going to have enough to live the lifestyle I want? Will I be able to retire when I plan to? How long will my money last? How do I factor in rising healthcare costs?

Women will inherit approximately $28.7 trillion in assets as a result of generational wealth transfers. Those who don't inherit will accumulate wealth through their own professional accomplishments. We make approximately 80% of family household buying decisions, including those related to banking and financial services. We are too powerful to be fearful. We need to be empowered to be effective decision-makers. So what do we need to do? Plan, plan, plan. It starts there.

Stomping out the fears

Many women have an unhealthy fear of investing. I understand what you're thinking: I could lose what I have and be unable to get it back. I don't really know what I'm doing. I don't understand the specifics of my investment choices. I lost a lot of money during the Great Recession. I feel I'm talked down to instead of engaged in the conversation about my investments. Fewer companies are sponsoring pension plans and who knows the future of Social Security. Your only way to build a nest egg is by investing. The reality is that you're still losing buying power because of inflation. Your money will not be worth in the future what it's worth today.

In the 1990s, a pair of high-end designer shoes cost around $400. Today, if you wanted to get a low-end designer shoe, the price starts at $700 and that could be a sale. Shoe prices have increased drastically. They are a hot commodity, giving rise to the success of designers such as Michael Kors. A few years ago his company, Michael Kors Holdings Limited, made its initial public

PRICES

A pair of Manolo Blahniks

In 1985 — $300

Today — $755

Average price for a house

In 1985 — $82K

Today — $300K

Average cost for a wedding

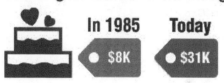

In 1985 — $8K

Today — $31K

offering (IPO) and now has a market capitalization of about $9.75 billion.

Fear, in any capacity, is natural. Too often we don't want to admit that we're afraid because we're supposed to have the answers, or we're called to be authoritative and brave. Admitting fear is actually a sign of strength. Addressing it is even more courageous. There's nothing wrong with having apprehension around your financial future—especially investing—but it's no excuse for not taking action. That's when empowerment and information intersect to diminish your fears and make you knowledgeable so you can move forward with certainty.

Let's take it from another perspective. As a child learning to walk, you decided you would take your very first series of steps. It didn't matter that you had fallen down many times before. You kept trying. The possibility of hurting yourself was there, but you kept trying. All you knew at the time was there was a better way for you to get to your destination, so you had to learn to use your legs. It was quicker once you got the hang of it. Investing is the adult version of that milestone. You may wobble. You will make mistakes (there's no maybe about it). External factors you have no control over—the political environment, world events, the economy—will affect your portfolio and its performance. I'm telling you, investing is a journey. Understand that the more you know, the less fear will grip you and the more confident you will feel. Then that internal confidence will show as you step out each day strutting in those red-bottom heels.

No plan is bulletproof, but it helps to sit down and discuss things with a professional, someone you feel you can trust. Explain where you are now and where you're trying to go. Describe how you envision your life after you retire from the 9-to-5. Discuss your current cash flow—your income minus your expenses—and any major changes you expect to face by the time you want to retire. Ask questions. Participating in the process and staying engaged helps develop confidence in where you are going financially.

As an investor, you can actively participate in the companies you own by becoming an advocate. As a shareholder advocate, you have the power to influence corporate governance decisions. One way is using your stock ownership to put pressure on a company's management to implement specific changes in how the company is run and its practices as a corporate citizen. Investors can engage in filing resolutions for shareholders' votes, attracting media attention to issues to improve company practices, litigation, or reaching out to companies to open a dialogue about changes that could improve performance, promote value, and have social impact.

I'm finding that there are more socially responsible investors (SRI) today, those who are looking for opportunities to invest in companies that have accountability when it comes to the environment, social justice, and corporate governance. These investors encourage companies to promote environmental stewardship, consumer protection, human rights, and/or diversity. Other investors want to avoid investments that are involved in specific industries such as alcohol, tobacco, weapons, gambling, fossil fuel, or pornography because these industries promote habits or behaviors that go against their core values. Instead, they choose to invest with their hearts.

CHAPTER 6

Passing Down the Pumps: Lessons for Our Daughters

I'm writing this during the season of college and high school graduations. The energy and excitement around these events make me think back to my own graduations, when I was so ready to go on to the next chapter of my life. (That's why, for me, wearing heels symbolizes adulthood, confidence, and being able to make my own choices. And on a totally superficial level, it meant I was elegant, classy, and sexy, especially after I learned how to strut in them.) All I could think, at both of my graduations, was "Now I am officially an adult." Of course, now I know that wasn't necessarily true, but you couldn't tell me that. I had my first job lined up, as an auditor at the Defense Logistics Agency, and I was heading to the Washington, D.C., area to make my mark.

All this reminiscing has me thinking ahead about my daughter's future, what I hope for her life and the dreams I have for her. But all those things can't and won't be accomplished without a plan. I'm starting to focus on her later years. When I make a plan, I look as far into the future as I can. One of my ideas for her is to have her work for me as a teenager and when she's in college, and I will use a portion of her earnings to open and fund a Roth IRA in her name. I feel this will give her a sense of responsibility and be a learning tool to further demonstrate finances and investing to her at a younger age than I was when I learned about them. It's important to prepare our children for their futures, particularly their financial futures.

Many years ago, a colleague shared a personal story about what her parents did to prepare her for her future. They decided to have just one child because when they factored their finances, they felt best limiting the growth of their family because they wanted to ensure their financial security. When I first heard the story, I was intrigued. It fascinated me that her parents thought so far in advance about the dynamics of their family and what that would consist of for them financially.

Here's what really impressed me: They started planning for her retirement when she was in college. Her father set up a Roth IRA and must have figured that by starting a retirement account when she was 18, she turned 65, she could accumulate more than $700,000 in retirement savings. At $3,000 per year, the accumulation would be well over $1 million. Talk about starting your child off on the right foot! This amazing story planted the seed for me to do the same for my child. I want my daughter to know the responsibility of earning her money and the freedom it can bring when managed properly.

Sending your daughter (and your money) to college

When your child starts the college application process, picks a school, and makes plans to leave your home, maybe for the first extended period of time, it's an emotional milestone. It's even more pivotal for young women than young men making the transition to the independent, self-sufficient life of a college girl. There's so much for her to learn—in class and in life—that it's exciting and overwhelming for any mother to think about. Good thing I have a few years to hold on to before I have to really start thinking about it, at least in the emotional sense. Financially, however, I've been contemplating it since she was an infant, even before she was ever born.

As much as I want our daughter to go to a wonderful school and get a great education, my husband and I agreed that we will not forgo our plans for retirement to fund her education. You may not agree with our approach. Some people don't. But I heard someone say recently—and I agree with the sentiment—I can't get a loan to retire, but my child can get a loan for her education. To alleviate retirement savings concerns, we decided to prepare early for college expenses by starting an education account immediately after she was born. That was also a lesson I learned from someone I know. A friend invited me to his son's dedication. In lieu of gifts, he asked everyone to give a donation to his son's college savings account. I thought that was a fabulous idea and I now share this idea with my clients. Because my grandma knows how important saving is to me, she only gives my daughter piggy banks of coins she accumulates during the year. To some it may not be much, but I appreciate the sentiment. She understands my values of putting money aside for my daughter's education. It's these subliminal messages that we think our kids don't see that helps create their money philosophy. It sticks with them throughout life.

There are many savings options available to parents, so to simplify the presentation of the various vehicles, I laid the information out in a chart to make it easier to read and process. (Please note that this is a high-level summary and doesn't include all the specific details of each option.)

TYPE OF ACCOUNT	BASIC INFORMATION	TAX CONSIDERATIONS	OTHER CONSIDERATIONS
CollegeSure CDs	Federally insured to $100,000; interest linked to annual increase in college costs.	Interest earned is taxable and early withdrawal penalty applies.	Principle and interest can be used for any purpose if the child does not go to college.
529 Prepaid and Savings Plans	Initial investment is minimal; annual contributions can be up to $28,000 if made jointly with a spouse, or $70,000 every 5 years for 529 savings plan; no income restrictions; parents purchase tuition credits for prepaid plan.	Earnings grow tax-deferred; qualified withdrawals are free from federal income tax.	Costs paid via a 529 plan cannot be used toward the Hope Scholarship or Lifetime Learning Credit. Assets in a 529 plan are included in federal financial aid calculations; with the prepaid plan you lock in the child's tuition rate years in advance.
Coverdell Education Savings Accounts (Education IRA)	Can only contribute $2,000 per year per child.	Earnings are not taxed as long as used for education expenses; transfers to siblings are not taxable.	Income limitations for high earners. May be used for elementary, secondary, and postsecondary education expenses; account balances can be transferred to siblings.
Insurance	Policy must accumulate a cash value (whole, universal life, or variable universal life).	Tax deferral on earnings; parents can borrow against the cash value of the policy, which is not a taxable event.	Access to funds can be relatively quick and no credit analysis is needed; life insurance is not considered in federal financial aid calculations; consider costs because insurance can be a more expensive option.
UTMA/ UGMA	A custodial account managed by the parent; considered the asset of the child.	Earnings and gains taxed at the child's rate.	The child gains access to account at age of majority; The child may have to contribute 20% of assets to college costs before he/she can apply for financial aid; cannot change owner.

Information obtained from AXA Equitable (http://www.axa-equitable.com/plan/educa-tion/529-plans/529.html), www.savingforcollege.com, and 4th Edition of Financial Planning: Process and Environment, chapter 8.

Of course, I recommend meeting with a financial professional to discuss your options. But before you schedule an appointment, you need to be clear about your goals. Here are a few questions to consider:

- Do you want your child to attend an in-state or out-of-state institution? In-state institutions cost significantly less than out-of-state institutions.
- Is this institution public or private?
- How much have you accumulated thus far?
- Are you going to pay for all or a portion of the costs?
- What amount are you planning to pay?
- Are you going to pay for graduate school?
- Is there additional funding coming from grandparents?
- Does your child own a savings or investment account?

This isn't a comprehensive list of questions, but it will *catalyze* the thinking that will create one.

Make your daughter an active partner in the funding
For her part, my eight-year-old daughter is learning the

importance of saving for her own education. As I mentioned earlier, my grandmother gives her a piggy bank full of silver coins each time we see her. She teases my daughter, telling her she is so smart that next year she's going to college (which supports and encourages my daughter in a completely different way). One day, I told my daughter we were going to use some of the money for pizza day at school, and she kindly told me no, we couldn't use it for that because it's for her education. I was surprised that she remembered the jokes my grandmother made because she never told her how to use the coins. She just saves them and gives them to her. I love that she recognizes that a college education isn't free and knows we have to save for it.

While I was shopping with my daughter recently, she mentioned a couple of items that she wanted: a soft pillow for staying at her favorite aunt's house, a book she could add to her collection. I told her that I wasn't buying both because I didn't want to spend money on them in addition to what I was purchasing that day, so she had to pick the one she wanted more. She reacted, of course. "Mommy, please let me get both," she begged. I was adamant that I was buying just one. She put on her pouty face to convince me to change my mind. I stood my ground. Finally, she selected one. My goal is for her to realize that everything has a price and we have to consider it when determining the amount we will spend on a trip to the store. I also want her to realize she can't have everything she wants just because she wants it.

I let her know when she asks for something that Mommy doesn't have the money for that item today. I don't believe in giving her a lot of "things," but what I do buy for her usually has an educational component. I believe in giving her experiences that she will always remember. I want her to embrace learning and exploring life.

I often think about the legacy I want to leave for my daughter. I want her to understand that money isn't everything but it gives her options. That's why it's important for her to value it. One of my duties as a parent is to teach financial principles that allow her to live a better life. I want her to understand that she needs to plan for the unexpected. Live below her means. Help those less fortunate. Never stop growing. Appreciate opportunities to learn. Find her passion. Save for emergencies. Invest for her future. Understand the importance of negotiation. Buy quality versus quantity. Learn the effective use of multiple streams of income. Leave a legacy for the next generation. You may want to pass down some of the same values to your children.

My goal with this book is to impart great information that's easy to understand, practical, and, most important, useful in your day-to-day financial life. I want it to change how you think about and view money, saving, and investing. I hope it helps you accept that you may make mistakes but feel consolation knowing that you can rebound from them. Your who come after you. That's why it's important to me for you to feel comfortable sharing this book with other women in your life, because you've used the information to help you get on your own path of financial success and believe it will greatly assist them, too. Finally, I want you to walk away from this book believing that you can achieve your financial goals, recognizing that it takes guidance, consistency, active engagement, and patience. Your success, just like this book, is part of my professional legacy. As you strut away in your pumps believing your goals are attainable, I want you to feel just as comfortable sharing this book as you would a great pair of shoes with your best friend.

Shoe Closet: Terms to Try On and Wear

*U*nderstanding these terms is just a way for me to equip you with pertinent information. Are they going to help you in your day-to-day life? Probably not. But they'll help you understand what may be going on with our economy and remove some of the fear as you hear these words thrown around on the news.

Annual Report: The comprehensive report of a company's activities for the previous year that's sent out to shareholders and prospective investors.

Bear Market: A declining stock market over a period of time, some say defined as a price decline of 20% or more over at least a two-month period. The 21st century bear market, otherwise known as the Great Recession, started October 9, 2007, and ended March 5, 2009. As many of you know, it has resulted in high unemployment and a major reduction in home values.

Bull Run: A sustained period of time when stock prices rise, the economy is strong, and unemployment is low. This term often makes our minds go back to the Clinton White House years. The stock market was rising, everyone was optimistic, jobs were plentiful, house prices rose in value, and no one appeared to be concerned with inflation.

Certified Financial Planner: A professional designation earned by financial planners who pass a 10-hour exam and have extensive experience in the financial planning field.

Compound Interest: When the interest you earned on an investment earns interest.

Double-dip: When the economy emerges from a recession, goes on to a brief surge of growth, but then falls back into a recession. This term is thrown around quite often in the financial news, and even on the local news, when anchors discuss the U.S. economy and the current volatility in the stock market.

Dow Jones Industrial Average: A price-weighted average of 30 large companies trading on the New York Stock Exchange and the NASDAQ Stock Market.

Environment, Social Justice, Governance (ESG): The three areas used to gauge the impact of a company's sustainable and ethical impact.

Exchange Traded Funds (ETFs): A marketable security that tracks an index like the Dow Jones, S&P 500, Wilshire 5000 (total stock market), or MSCI EAFE Index (foreign stocks in Europe, Australasia, and the Far East). ETFs trade like stocks, meaning they have daily liquidity. They generally have lower internal fees than mutual funds.

Gross Domestic Product: The dollar value of all the finished goods and services produced within a country during a specific time period, generally annually.

Inflation: The sustained increased cost of goods and services over time.

Initial Public Offering (IPO): The first sale of a private company's stock to the public. You may remember the hype around the Facebook and Twitter IPOs.

Market Capitalization: The dollar value of the shares a company has outstanding.

Market Correction: Sometimes referred to as a "mini-bear" market, this term is used when the Dow Jones and S&P 500 estimate that markets are dropping by 10%–20%. These indices measure how well the best companies in America are performing financially.

Mutual Fund: An investment that utilizes a pool of funds from investors to purchase a selection of securities such as stocks, bonds, and money market instruments.

NASDAQ Stock Market: The second-largest U.S. stock exchange. It's the world's first electronic stock market.

New York Stock Exchange: Known as the Big Board, it's the world's largest stock exchange by market capitalization, headquartered in New York City.

Nonfarm Payroll Report: The jobs report is released by the Department of Labor the first Friday of every month and provides the previous month's employment information. After its release, this report can and often does affect the markets.

Proxy Statement: Used to solicit votes from shareholders, this document is sent out prior to a company's annual meeting. It's also filed with the U.S. Securities and Exchange Commission.

Recession: A long period of falling economic activity as measured by the gross domestic product (GDP) for two successive quarters. Actually, a recession is a normal, although unpleasant, part of the business cycle. What the country experienced in 2008 has been referred to as the Great Recession.

Roth IRA: An individual retirement account in which you contribute after-tax income up to the IRS-specified yearly amount. Once you allow your account to grow for at least five years leading up to age 59½, earnings withdrawn are tax-free.

Rule of 72: A method for estimating how long it will take for an investment to double. Take the number 72 and divide by the annual rate of return you earn. For a precise answer use a financial calculator, but it's useful for approximating.

S&P 500: An index that represents the market capitalization of 500 of the largest companies listed on the New

York Stock Exchange and the NASDAQ Stock Market. Also known as Standard & Poor's 500.

Social Responsible Investing (SRI): Sustainable, ethical, socially, and environmentally conscious investing. It seeks financial growth while considering a social cause.

Traditional IRA: An individual retirement account in which you are allowed to contribute before- and after-tax dollars. Your money grows tax-deferred, and you pay no taxes until you make a withdrawal. Withdrawals generally made prior to age 59½ are subject to a 10% penalty, and all withdrawals are treated as current income.

Volatility: The measurement of the variation of price for an investment over a period of time. With investments, the higher the volatility, the riskier it is.

529 Plan: A tax-advantage vehicle that allows savings toward the future higher-education needs of a designated beneficiary such as a child, grandchild, or sibling.

10-K: The annual report that a publicly traded company must submit to the U.S. Securities and Exchange Commission. The report provides a comprehensive overview of a company's financials and audited financial statements.

10-Q: The quarterly report that publicly traded companies must file with the U.S. Securities and Exchange Commission. The information provided is less detailed than a 10-K and includes unaudited financial statements.

Resources: *To Style Your Shoe Wardrobe*

Tools for Women Business Owners

1) Small Business Administration
   (www.sba.gov/sizeup)
2) Chase Mission Main Street Grants (www.mis-
   sionmainstreetgrants.com)
3) Women's Business Enterprise National Council (www.wbenc.org)
4) National Association of Women Business
   Owners (www.nawbo.org)
5) American Business Women's Association
   (www.abwa.org)
6) America's Small Business Summit
   (www.uschamber.com/event)

Financial Apps

1) Expensify.com: Keeps track of business travel expenses.

2) Mint.com: Tracks account balances and helps you maintain your budget with notifications when you are going off-track.

3) Paypal.com: Allows businesses and individuals to receive payments from clients and pay for items in lieu of using a credit card. For entrepreneurs, this can be another source for building credit and accessing capital.

4) Acorns.com: Lets you quickly and automatically invest small amounts of money for those who desire to invest more.

5) Homebudget (www.anishu.com/index.html): Expense-management application that allows you to sync your budget to your mobile device for easy tracking.

6) Billguard.com: Monitors account activity for fraud.

7) SavedPlus.com: Allows you to set up savings based on a percentage of each purchase you make.

8) Bankrate.com: Personal finance site that aggregates rate information on various financial

instruments and provides collective financial information for consumers.

Conferences for Women

1) National Association for Female Executives Conference (www.workingmother.com/conference-events/womens-leadership-summits/events)

2) Annual Women's Leadership Conference (www.conference-board.org)

3) Women's Business Enterprise National Council National Conference and Business Fair (conf.wbenc.org)

4) Diversity Woman Conference (diversity-woman.com)

5) Black Enterprise Women's Conference (www.blackenterprise.com/events/women-of-power-summit)

6) Forbes Women's Summit (www.forbesconferences.com)

7) Fortune Most Powerful Women Summit (www.fortuneconferences.com)

8) TEDWomen (www.ted.com/attend/conferences/special-events/tedwomen)

9) National Women's Business Conference

hosted by the National Association of Women Business Owners (www.nawbo.org)

10) American Small Business Summit (www.uschamber.com)

References

1) Financial Services Industry in the United States. (n.d.). Retrieved from Select USA: selectusa .commerce.gov/industry-snap-shots/financial-services-industry-united-states

2) One in 8 workers will never retire. (2013, 9 18). Retrieved from CNN Money: http://money.cnn.com/2013/09/18/retire-ment/workers-never-retire/index.html

3) Women Investors: Four Tips. (2014, May 22). Retrieved from Fidelity Viewpoints: https://www.fidelity.com/viewpoints/per-sonal-finance/investing-tips-for-women

4) Medicare.gov. (n.d.). Retrieved from skilled nursing facility (SNF) care: https://www.medicare.gov/coverage/skilled-nursing-facility-care.html

5) Find Your Perfect Engagement Ring. (n.d.). Retrieved from Tiffany & Co: http://www.tiffany.com/Shopping/Default.aspx?mcat=148203

6) Love and Money — By the Numbers. (2014, June 1). Retrieved from Money: http://time.com/money/2800576/love-money-by-the-numbers/

7) The Knot, The #1 Wedding Site, Releases 2014 Real Weddings Study Statistics. (2015, March 12). Retrieved from The Knot: http://www.xogroupinc.com/press-releases-home/2015-press-releases/2015-03-12-the-knot-2014-real-weddings-study.aspx

8) Rock, C. (2004). Never Scared. (C. Rock, Performer) Constitution Hall, Washington, DC, U.S.

9) Taylor, A. (Director). (2002). Sex in the City: Ring a Ding Ding [Sitcom]

10) Viacom pays $2.3B for BET . (2000, 11 3). Retrieved from Money.CNN.com: http://money.cnn.com/2000/11/03/deals/viacom/